For

JANUARY

The Birthstone Petite Collection

By Suzanne Siegel Zenkel

Design and illustration by
Mullen and Katz

PETER PAUPER PRESS, INC.
WHITE PLAINS · NEW YORK

*Special thanks to
Lois L. Kaufman and
Claudine Gandolfi for their
editorial assistance*

Copyright © 1996
Peter Pauper Press, Inc.
202 Mamaroneck Avenue
White Plains, NY 10601
ISBN 0-88088-975-6
Printed in China
7 6 5 4 3 2 1

Contents

A Month Like No Other

❧

January Celebrities
and What They
Have to Say

❧

Parties, Cakes,
Candles, Flowers, and
Birthstones

January
A Month Like No Other

Your birthstone is the
Garnet

And your special flower is the
Carnation

Ring out the old, ring in the new,
Ring, happy bells, across the snow;
The year is going, let him go;
Ring out the false, ring in the true.

Alfred, Lord Tennyson

What could be better than bringing in the New Year with your birthday? What joy to have millions celebrate with you! No month of the year rivals January for its sweet anticipation of what the future holds. January represents beginnings—the opening of gates to the future. The month ushers in the promise of a fresh start for all, but especially for those celebrating January birthdays.

January is rich with important historical events, not the least of which is the British Calendar Act of 1751, which set the beginning of each New Year on January First in most English-speaking countries. Abraham Lincoln issued the Emancipation Proclamation on January 1, 1863, declaring all slaves in the Confederacy "forever free." Thirty years later, another "gateway to freedom" opened its doors, on January 1, 1892, at the immigration center on Ellis Island. Martin Luther King Day is observed as a holiday on the Monday nearest to his January 15th birth date. Thomas Alva Edison was granted the first patent for his incandescent bulb on January 27, 1880, bringing new light to the world. Enrico Caruso's singular voice was heard on January 3, 1900, during the world's first public radio broadcast. And on January 5, 1993, the greatest number of female representatives in history was sworn into the U. S. Congress.

January also encompasses happenings that may be considered quirky or important, depending on who's doing the considering—the annual Polar Bear Swim, for one! Every New Year's Day hardy swimmers (and dunkers) go for a frosty dip in the waters of places like Lake Michigan and Coney Island, NY. An event of greater cultural significance occurred on January 8, 1935—the birth of Elvis Presley, King of Rock 'n' Roll. Despite his 1977 death, the King's music continues to reign supreme and his fans continue to adore him. The "British (musical) invasion" began on January 13, 1964, with the American release of *I Want to Hold Your Hand*, by the Beatles. On an even sweeter note, the beloved Chocolate Chip Cookie also has a

January birthday. What a recipe for success this was! On January 15, 1939, the first such delicacy rolled out of Ruth Wakefield's oven at Toll House Inn in Whitman, Massachusetts, bringing about a mouth-watering new national passion. And January is the perfect month for those who want something to go with their cookies, when we celebrate National Hot Tea Month, National Soup Month, and National Prune Breakfast Month, perhaps while watching the "Today" Show, which debuted on January 14, 1952.

January has an eclectic roster of people born within its thirty-one days. Even more interesting is what they have to say! So, turn the pages, January babies, and delight in the wit and wisdom of your fellow birthday honorees!

January Celebrities and What They Have to Say

January 1

PAUL REVERE, 1735

BETSY ROSS, 1752

E. M. FORSTER, 1879

BARRY GOLDWATER, 1909

January 1

I think writing is a hard life.
But it's brought me enough
happiness that I don't think I'd
ever deliberately dissuade anybody
(if he had talent) from taking it up.
The compensations are few, but
when they come, if they come,
they're very beautiful.

J. D. SALINGER, 1919

January 2

ISAAC ASIMOV, 1920

ROGER MILLER, 1936

JOHN IRVING, 1942

DAVID CONE, 1963

January 3

J. R. R. TOLKIEN, 1892

RAY MILLAND, 1905

DABNEY COLEMAN, 1932

As long as my body is in shape, my
mind works at its full capacity.
VICTORIA PRINCIPAL, 1950

MEL GIBSON, 1956

January 4

SIR ISAAC NEWTON, 1643
JANE WYMAN, 1914

You have to feel the disappointments, heartaches and losses to be able to move on. You put so much time into it, you can't ever feel it too deeply. You've got to feel it down to your bones.

DON SHULA, 1930

DYAN CANNON, 1937

January 5

WALTER F. MONDALE, 1928
ALVIN AILEY, 1931
ROBERT DUVALL, 1931

I personally feel that I want to
have my own life and work and be
with somebody who thinks of me
as an equal, you know, and that's
important for everybody.
DIANE KEATON, 1946

January 6

JOAN OF ARC, 1412
CAPT. JOHN SMITH, 1580
CARL SANDBURG, 1878

The soul is mightier than space,
stronger than time, deeper than the
sea, and higher than the stars.
KAHLIL GIBRAN, 1883

January 6

LORETTA YOUNG, 1913

DANNY THOMAS, 1914

E. L. DOCTOROW, 1931

NANCY LOPEZ, 1957

January 7

CHARLES ADDAMS, 1912

VINCENT GARDENIA, 1922

KENNY LOGGINS, 1948

KATIE COURIC, 1957

NICHOLAS CAGE, 1964

January 8

JOSE FERRER, 1912
CHARLES OSGOOD, 1933

Do what's right for you,
as long as it don't hurt no one.
ELVIS PRESLEY, 1935

CAROLINA HERRERA, 1939
STEPHEN HAWKING, 1942
DAVID BOWIE, 1947

January 9

SIMONE DE BEAUVOIR, 1908

The secret to a long life is never
look back, look forward. You've got
to have something to live for,
otherwise you cease to live.
RICHARD NIXON, 1913

January 9

FERNANDO LAMAS, 1915

JUDITH KRANTZ, 1928

BOB DENVER, 1935

JOAN BAEZ, 1941

CRYSTAL GAYLE, 1951

January 10

RAY BOLGER, 1904

SAL MINEO, 1939

JIM CROCE, 1943

ROD STEWART, 1945

GEORGE FOREMAN, 1949

PAT BENATAR, 1953

January 11

ALEXANDER HAMILTON, 1755
ROD TAYLOR, 1929

I think the best way to predict the future is to create it. . . . I'm just real prayerful right now. I know that God has a plan for me. And I'm living fully in the moment. My motto these days is *Slow down, simplify, and be kind.*

NAOMI JUDD, 1946

January 11

I'm six foot eleven.
My birthday covers three days.
DARRYL DAWKINS, 1957

January 12

JOHN SINGER SARGENT, 1856
JACK LONDON, 1876
HENNY YOUNGMAN, 1906

January 12

Pioneers take the arrows.
If you take a stand with cockiness
and bravado, like I do, you've got
to expect people to fire back. But
you can't let yourself be intimidated
out of what you truly feel.

RUSH LIMBAUGH, 1941

HOWARD STERN, 1954
KIRSTIE ALLEY, 1955

January 13

ROBERT STACK, 1919

GWEN VERDON, 1925

CHARLES NELSON REILLY, 1931

I don't know where I'll end up,
but I'm doing what I would like to
do in many aspects of my life. . . .
So that's nice.
JULIA LOUIS-DREYFUS, 1962

January 14

BERTHE MORISOT, 1841

It is through the idealism
of youth that man catches sight
of truth, and in that idealism he
possesses a wealth which he must
never exchange for anything else.

ALBERT SCHWEITZER, 1875

January 14

You never get used to your age,
no matter what age you are.
The trouble is, you're that age
for such a short time. Just when you
begin to get used to it, you get
a year older.

ANDY ROONEY, 1919

FAYE DUNAWAY, 1941

January 15

ARISTOTLE ONASSIS, 1906

LLOYD BRIDGES, 1913

CARDINAL JOHN J. O'CONNOR, 1920

January 15

I have a dream.
It is a dream deeply rooted in
the American dream. I have a
dream that one day this nation
will rise up and live out the true
meaning of its creed.
MARTIN LUTHER KING, JR., 1929

MARGARET O'BRIEN, 1937
SADE, 1960

January 16

ETHEL MERMAN, 1909

FRANCESCO SCAVULLO, 1929

SUSAN SONTAG, 1933

DEBBIE ALLEN, 1950

January 17

I should have no objection
to go over the same life from its
beginning to the end: requesting
only the advantage authors have,
of correcting in a second edition the
faults of the first.

BENJAMIN FRANKLIN, 1706

January 17

BETTY WHITE, 1924

JAMES EARL JONES, 1931

SHARI LEWIS, 1934

The man who views the world
at 50 the same as he did at
20 has wasted 30 years of his life.
MUHAMMAD ALI, 1942

ANDY KAUFMAN, 1949

DAVID CARUSO, 1956

PAUL YOUNG, 1956

January 18

But now I'm six,
I'm clever as clever
So I think I'll be six
for ever and ever.
A. A. MILNE, 1882,
Now We Are Six

OLIVER HARDY, 1892
CARY GRANT, 1904
DANNY KAYE, 1913
KEVIN COSTNER, 1955

January 19

ROBERT E. LEE, 1807

EDGAR ALLEN POE, 1809

PAUL CEZANNE, 1839

JEAN STAPLETON, 1923

JANIS JOPLIN, 1943

January 19

The longer I live,
the more apparent it becomes
to me that paradise is not a goal at
the end of the road, but the road
itself. . . . More important than the
road itself are the people we meet
along the way. That is the
real key to life.

DOLLY PARTON, 1946

January 20

I smoke cigars because
at my age if I don't have something
to hang onto I might fall down.
GEORGE BURNS, 1896

ANSEL ADAMS, 1902

JOY ADAMSON, 1910

PATRICIA NEAL, 1926

EDWIN E. "BUZZ" ALDRIN, 1930

LORENZO LAMAS, 1958

January 21

CHRISTIAN DIOR, 1905
TELLY SAVALAS, 1925

The older you get
the stronger the wind gets—
and it's always in your face.
JACK NICKLAUS, 1940

PLACIDO DOMINGO, 1941
JILL EIKENBERRY, 1947
ROBBY BENSON, 1956
GEENA DAVIS, 1957

January 22

LORD BYRON, 1788

ANN SOTHERN, 1909

PIPER LAURIE, 1932

BILL BIXBY, 1934

JOSEPH WAMBAUGH, 1937

JOHN HURT, 1940

JAMIE LEE CURTIS, 1958

January 23

EDOUARD MANET, 1832

RANDOLPH SCOTT, 1898

ERNIE KOVACS, 1919

January 23

RICHARD DEAN ANDERSON, 1953

PRINCESS CAROLINE OF
MONACO, 1957

HAKEEM OLAJUWON, 1963

January 24

EDITH WHARTON, 1862

ERNEST BORGNINE, 1917

AVA GARDNER, 1922

NEIL DIAMOND, 1941

JOHN BELUSHI, 1949

You can do extraordinary things
if you rise above your limits,
both real and imaginary.

MARY LOU RETTON, 1968

January 25

ROBERT BURNS, 1759

One of the signs of passing youth is
the birth of a sense of fellowship
with other human beings as we
take our place among them.
VIRGINIA WOOLF, 1882

CORAZON AQUINO, 1933
LEIGH TAYLOR-YOUNG, 1944
DINAH MANOFF, 1958

January 26

DOUGLAS MACARTHUR, 1880
MARIA VON TRAPP, 1905

What I would really like to put
on my tombstone is that I was part
of my time. And I'm satisfied with
that. And that's comforting.
I did okay. It's been good.
PAUL NEWMAN, 1925

EARTHA KITT, 1928
GENE SISKEL, 1946

January 26

ANITA BAKER, 1958

You miss 100 percent of the shots
you never take.
WAYNE GRETZKY, 1961

January 27

WOLFGANG AMADEUS
MOZART, 1756

LEWIS CARROLL, 1832

JEROME KERN, 1885

DONNA REED, 1921

MIKHAIL BARYSHNIKOV, 1948

January 28

To be astonished
is one of the surest ways of not
growing old too quickly.
COLETTE, 1873

JACKSON POLLOCK, 1912
SUSAN SONTAG, 1933
ALAN ALDA, 1936

January 29

THOMAS PAINE, 1737

W. C. FIELDS, 1880

JOHN FORSYTHE, 1918

January 29

Women over fifty already form
one of the largest groups in the
population structure of the western
world. As long as they like themselves, they will not be an oppressed
minority. In order to like themselves
they must reject trivialization by
others of who and what they are.

GERMAINE GREER, 1939

TOM SELLECK, 1945

January 29

ANN JILLIAN, 1950

I am a woman in progress.
I'm just trying, like everyone else.
I try to take every conflict, every
experience, and learn from it.
All I know is that I can't be
anybody else. And it's taken me a
long time to realize that.
OPRAH WINFREY, 1954

GREG LOUGANIS, 1960

January 30

First of all, let me assert my firm
belief that the only thing we have to
fear is fear itself . . .
FRANKLIN D. ROOSEVELT, 1882

GENE HACKMAN, 1930
TAMMY GRIMES, 1934
VANESSA REDGRAVE, 1937

January 31

TALLULAH BANKHEAD, 1903

A life is not important except in
the impact it has on others.
JACKIE ROBINSON, 1919

CAROL CHANNING, 1923
NORMAN MAILER, 1923
SUZANNE PLESHETTE, 1937
RICHARD GEPHARDT, 1941

January 31

My basic philosophy of life
came from my parents: Treat people
the way you want to be treated,
with honesty and integrity.
NOLAN RYAN, 1947

PHIL COLLINS, 1951

Parties, Cakes, Candles, Flowers, and Birthstones

Happy Birthday to You

It should come as no surprise that *Happy Birthday to You* is commonly referred to as "the most frequently sung number in the world." After all, a birthday is one of the few things in life that we all have.

Birthdays mean different things to each of us. When we were children, most of us regarded our birthday with boundless excitement, reveling in our chance to be the focus of attention. To adults, birthdays evoke an enormous range of sentiments, awakening for some of us excitement reminiscent of childhood. Others spend their birthdays reflecting on the events of the passing years or anticipating what the future holds. Yet, no matter how we regard our birthday at a given time, we all feel a certain response to the day. And from time immemorial, one of the very best ways to celebrate a birthday has been to throw a party and have a ball!

Life's a Party

How did birthday parties come to be? The first to throw birthday parties were the ancient Europeans. In those days, people believed strongly in the power of good and evil spirits, and how the evil spirits might prey on a birthday celebrant was unknown. Family and friends would gather 'round the celebrant in order to ward off any evil spirits. Thus, the origins of the first birthday party, replete with good wishes and cheer, were thought to be to protect the celebrant from any mysterious dangers a birthday might present.

Birthday gifts were believed to offer even greater protection from evil spirits. People also reveled in games and fun as a symbol of bidding farewell to the past year and bringing in the new year with joy. In the earliest days, birthday parties were planned for only the most prominent in the community. As time evolved, the custom was shared by common people and eventually children's birthdays became the most celebrated of all. So, birthday parties were first fashioned in order to assure the next year's good fortune.

Have Your Cake and Eat It, Too!

Who first cooked up the idea of a birthday cake? The ancient Greeks believed in Artemis, Goddess of the Moon. In celebration of her birthday, they would bring round, moon-shaped cakes to her temple. Birthday cakes are often round, reminiscent of this custom. In the United States, there has evolved another tradition—that of having the celebrant cut the first slice.

Don't Burn the Candle at Both Ends!

Why the old flame at your birthday party? The first to use lighted candles on birthday cakes were the Germans. The birthday celebrant silently made a wish and then blew out the flames. The wish would be granted only if all the candles were blown out in one puff. The custom to have one candle for each year evolved from this tradition, and in the United States and elsewhere, one candle "to grow on" has been added.

Older Grown

The days are gone,
The months have flown,
And you and I are older grown.
Shake hands, good-bye,
and have no fear
To welcome well another year.

KATE GREENAWAY

Say It with Flowers!

Each month has a special flower associated with it.

Month	Flower
JANUARY	CARNATION
FEBRUARY	PRIMROSE
MARCH	DAFFODIL
APRIL	DAISY
MAY	LILY OF THE VALLEY
JUNE	ROSE
JULY	LARKSPUR
AUGUST	GLADIOLUS
SEPTEMBER	ASTER
OCTOBER	DAHLIA
NOVEMBER	CHRYSANTHEMUM
DECEMBER	POINSETTIA

You're a Gem!

The most widely embraced of the customs associated with birthdays is the wearing of the birthstone—the gemstone which symbolizes the month of your birth. In ancient times, people believed that good luck would be brought to a person wearing his or her birthstone. Many also believed that wearing one's birthstone strengthened character. The following lists the gems generally accepted as the birthstone for each month.

Month	Stone
JANUARY	GARNET
FEBRUARY	AMETHYST
MARCH	AQUAMARINE
APRIL	DIAMOND
MAY	EMERALD
JUNE	PEARL
JULY	RUBY
AUGUST	PERIDOT
SEPTEMBER	SAPPHIRE
OCTOBER	TOURMALINE/OPAL
NOVEMBER	TOPAZ
DECEMBER	TURQUOISE/ZIRCON